Hidden Mind of Freedom

A joyful, balanced way of living
is our natural response to being.

Hidden Mind
of Freedom

Tarthang Tulku

Dharma Publishing

 NYINGMA PSYCHOLOGY SERIES

Reflections of Mind
Gesture of Balance
Openness Mind
Kum Nye Relaxation, Parts 1 and 2
Skillful Means
Hidden Mind of Freedom

LIBRARY OF CONGRESS CATALOGING IN PUBLICATION DATA

Tarthang Tulku.
  Hidden mind of freedom.

  (Nyingma psychology series)
  Includes index.
  1. Religious life (Buddhism)   I. Title.   II. Series.
BQ4302.T37   294.3'444   81–17466
ISBN 0-913546-82-8   AACR2
ISBN 0-913546-83-6 (pbk.)

Illustration and Design by Dharma Publishing

Typeset in Fototronic Palatino and Goudy Bold, printed,
and bound by Dharma Press, Oakland, California

9   8   7   6   5   4   3   2

The deep relaxation and openness of meditation offer a different perspective on our thoughts and perceptions. Meditation shows that we do not need to grasp at some experiences and reject others. We can accept all our experience, whether positive or negative. And this acceptance can lead to a deep satisfaction, a hearty appreciation of being alive. A new mind arises, bearing a sense of lightness and calm that ripples throughout all our activities like laughter.

*Dedicated to all who are
interested in the spiritual path*

Contents

Preface

From 1974 to 1976 I taught introductory classes in Buddhism at the Nyingma Institute in Berkeley, California. Over a period of several years, edited transcripts of some of these lectures appeared in *Crystal Mirror* and *Gesar* magazine, two periodicals produced by Dharma Publishing. About two years ago, Sylvia Derman, the editor of *Gesar*, suggested that the articles be gathered, reworked, and published as a book. Since it seemed that such a volume could be helpful to people interested in meditation and self-development, publication of *Hidden Mind of Freedom* was begun.

Working closely together, Sylvia and I collected the original papers and carefully reviewed and revised the resulting manuscript. In the final stages of preparation, Steve Randall, Jack Petranker, and other members of the staff of Dharma Publishing also assisted with the work, focusing on making the manuscript more cohesive and readable. I am deeply appreciative of all the efforts made by my students and friends at Dharma Publishing and Dharma Press in the editing and production of this book.

Hidden Mind of Freedom is not intended as a definitive discussion of the path to enlightenment. It is my hope that the suggestions made here will stimulate a quality of lightness and ease in your daily life, and encourage your efforts to explore the potential of mind. The mind is more than the thoughts it entertains; underneath lies a vital energy that is active, responsive, and attentive to every moment. Contacting this energy directly generates a sense of true enjoyment and satisfaction that enables us to appreciate all of our experience.

We live in a world that is crowded and frustrating, and it is often easy to forget that the peace within our mind is our only true refuge. May the passages of this book serve as reminders of the clarity and freedom of the awakened mind, calling us to our natural home.

Tarthang Tulku
November, 1981

Introduction

ⓜ editation is the foundation of self-development and well-being. Gradually, almost imperceptibly, meditation transforms the quality of everyday life, stimulating creativity, exercising mental capacities, and integrating body and mind. As awareness increases, we contact an inner source of fulfillment that enriches every moment of our experience.

Through meditation, we can open ourselves to a path of self-knowledge that leads ultimately to enlightenment. This path was taken twenty-five hundred years ago by the Buddha: his penetrating investigation into the causes of unhappiness and the means to perfect health culminated in the full realization of human potential. After his liberation, the Buddha taught that the highest realization is available to all of us, no matter what our background or present lifestyle—and unlike ordinary experience or achievement, this awareness cannot fade or lose its value with the passage of time.

The teachings of the Buddha invite us to develop our knowing capacity to the fullest and provide us with methods we can use in transforming everyday experience. A number of different meditation approaches may be found in this book, including breathing, mantra, and visualization practices. You can explore them all until you find those that best suit you; although the practices take different forms, each approach leads toward realization of the enlightened mind.

Understanding of the mind is at the heart of all Eastern philosophies and religions. They suggest that our experience comes *from* the mind, *by means of* the mind, and *for* the mind, and urge us to develop this understanding within our own lives. Since, for most of us, insight will arise only with the step-by-step transformation of our experience, we need to encourage ourselves to learn from everything we do. Firm confidence in experience itself is especially important in these times because there are so few genuine spiritual teachers available to guide us.

We can develop a close, reliable friendship with our experience. As this friendship grows, we discover that transcendence is not found somewhere beyond, or in some other time: whatever happens in our lives can serve to embody enlightenment. Even the density of confusion and pain can be transmuted into contemplation and fullness. We need simply to relax, allow our breathing to become calm, and watch our experience mindfully, without judgment. In this way we learn to foster lightness, joy, and compassion in our lives instead of resistance and disappointment. As meditation develops, we become naturally cheerful and find meaning in whatever we do.

How do you know when you have attained the highest realization? Sometimes after students have had an experience they consider enlightenment, they ask their teachers what to do next. But when you are free, you do not ask what to do or what not to do. Liberation is perfect knowledge of the truth, unobscured by judgments of right or wrong. Once we are enlightened, we participate continuously in the perfection of being.

Gaining a wider perspective is like opening a window in a stuffy room—the whole atmosphere changes and the fresh breeze carries alternatives to our habitual ways of reacting. Through the practice of self-observation in meditation and daily life, even our deepest questions can be answered. We can find out who we are and what we are doing on this earth. Ultimately, we may contact a body of knowledge so extensive that it touches everything.

ONE

Meditation

Meditation
and Relaxation

As relaxation deepens, the quality of
our inner awareness comes closer to
our natural state of mind.

editation allows us to contact our pure nature directly, and discover the awakened quality that is always there, at every moment of our lives. In the beginning we may think of meditation as something outside ourselves—an experience to be gained, a habit to acquire, or a discipline to master. But meditation is not external, it is within our mind: all the mind's nature can be our meditation.

Even if we have not practiced meditation, each of us has been inspired at times by strongly positive feelings that bring deep satisfaction. In meditation, we can learn to pay attention to such feelings, to communicate fully with them, and to cultivate and expand them. As the feelings of joy and pleasure intrinsic to meditation develop, the mind, alert and interested, naturally wants to continue.

It is best to begin simply and in a natural way, by sitting quietly and relaxing. The lotus position is excellent for meditation, but it is not necessary; you can use any comfortable posture in which your back is straight without being rigid. If you sit on the floor, a firm pillow will help keep your spine upright and take pressure off your thighs. Your hands can rest lightly on your knees or in your lap, whichever feels more natural. Let your eyes stay slightly open, focusing loosely a few feet ahead.

Begin with your body, letting go completely so that you are very, very relaxed. Relax your eyes, your forehead, the back of your neck, your hands. As much as you possibly can, let your body become soft, gentle, and loose. Let yourself become so sensitive that you can feel the pulse of your blood.

As you sit, let your breathing become very slow, very even and soft, like a gentle breeze or a slight wave on calm water. Bring your awareness to the breath, gently touching its feeling and quality. This is not a strict or formal observing, such as we might use when counting breaths, but a light, open awareness that contacts the breath directly and stimulates a quality of evenness within it.

Watch how the quality of your breathing changes as you focus your attention more fully. Continue without expectations or analysis until you touch a level where awareness merges with the breath. Though you have done nothing to change the quality of the breath, you will find that it has become calm and still. Thoughts move more slowly, and you can listen to the silence within your mind. A kind of warmth arises, a tangible feeling of relaxation that soothes and nourishes both body and mind.

Thus meditation begins by relaxing and letting everything become tranquil. When the breath grows calm, energy flows smoothly through the body and senses, balancing our inner circulation. As mental and bodily patterns soften, the quality of our inner awareness comes closer to our natural state of mind, which is open and accepting.

Sooner or later, however, a voice will surface and begin to create disturbances, thinking thoughts and evaluating our experience. Watch such thoughts and feelings as they rise to your attention, but don't follow these bubbles: let them be and they will pop. Be like an old woman watching a children's game. Though interested, she is calm and knowing, having been through it all before.

houghts take many forms, and you can learn to relax all of them. But neither try to *do* anything with them, nor try *not* to do anything with them. It is paradoxical yet true that any such efforts only create more thoughts and tension.

There is a story that illustrates how attempting to enforce silence actually disrupts meditation. In summertime, a flock of geese flew north to raise their families. When it began to get cold, they decided to return to a warmer climate. As they were preparing for their winter journey, one of the birds said, "Tonight we have to fly back, but everyone needs to fly very quietly; otherwise harm may come to us." So on the journey each bird said to the next one, "Quiet," until everyone was saying, "Quiet, quiet, quiet," and it became much noisier than before.

It is best to remain neutral toward thoughts no matter what happens. When we follow them, believing that they are solid or real and that they relate to some absolute category of good or bad, right or wrong, they multiply and disturb our peace of mind. Suppose, for example, that I think of my birthday and imagine that I will be given a wonderful present. Pleasant tinglings of emotion arise, and this one thought splinters into dozens of thoughts about my imaginary gift. They in turn arouse further emotions and thoughts. Like clowns climbing up on each others' shoulders, thoughts stack up in patterns held together by emotion.

Such interweavings of thoughts and emotions form the fabric of our everyday existence. Our mind creates the world in which we live, molding routines, desires, and expectations that are very solid and real to us. We are so habituated to this creation that we may find we cannot let go of it; we cannot go back to our intrinsic nature, to simple, direct experience.

The deep relaxation and openness of meditation offer a different perspective on our thoughts and perceptions. Meditation shows that we do not need to grasp at some experiences and reject others. We can accept all our experience, whether positive or negative. And this acceptance can lead to a deep satisfaction, a hearty appreciation of being alive. As our awareness and our response to living reflect the rich balance of meditation, our particular difficulties yield to a growing sense of confidence and enjoyment. A new mind arises, bearing a sense of lightness and calm that ripples throughout all our activities like laughter.

Self-Observation

*Self-observation is the
clear-sighted and wholesome mobilization
of all our resources and skills.*

The practice of self-observation in meditation and in daily life was perfected by the Buddha. A master of inner knowledge, the Enlightened One thoroughly examined all aspects of the mind. He explored the causes of suffering and revealed the way to transcend them and attain the highest realization. His teachings point the way to self-discovery, and urge us to learn for ourselves how the mind works. There is no knowledge greater than this.

As we set out on the path of direct observation, what do we find? First we discover a chaotic inner world of thoughts, concepts, images, and emotions. There is an endless round of inner interpretation, speculation, and discussion. Thoughts follow one after another, holding us tight with the power of the feelings and emotions they evoke. In time we may discern a pervasive web of confusion and unhappiness, a seemingly unbreakable pat-

tern of compulsion and habit. And even after we become aware of these processes, the flow of thoughts
and the habits they perpetuate continue apparently without pause.

Looking at our experience more deeply, we see that
this ceaseless activity neither solves our problems nor
satisfies our needs. In fact, the more we are caught up in
our thoughts and emotions, the more our energy is
drained and the farther we are led away from real
knowledge and insight. We may wonder what these
patterns are that have such power over us. Who is in
control of this flow of thoughts? Who is responsible for
maintaining our habits? If there is pain and confusion in
our minds, why do we accept it without question?

The answers to these questions will not necessarily
come at once. Seeing the mind clearly through its clouds
of activity can be difficult, like trying to find a fish in a
shadowy stream. Therefore, we must approach the mind
sensitively, and persevere in our efforts to understand it.
If we seek answers impatiently, demanding immediate
improvement in our situation, we may undermine the
attempt at self-discovery and become unable to find our
way. With such a hasty approach, awareness cannot be
cultivated, because there is no place for meditation to
take root. If we are tense, or caught up in emotions and
feeling frustrated, it is better simply to relax, forget about
our questions and problems, and concentrate on our
immediate experience.

Even if our initial attempts at self-observation
through meditation are discouraging and frustrating, we
need not lose heart. Growing familiarity with our mental

patterns and the suffering they create promotes our willingness to change. And at the same time that we see our negative qualities, we begin to appreciate the mind's ability to enrich and clarify our experience. Meditation can enable us to tap the healing qualities of mind, eventually transforming our impoverishing patterns of thought and action into liberating growth.

Merely thinking about the mind's potential, however, will not bring about change, for the intellect alone does not have the power to resolve our problems. Self-observation is not just a process of introspective analysis and interpretation; it is the clear-sighted and wholesome mobilization of all our resources and skills.

K een mindfulness throughout daily activities—not just during periods of formal meditation—will help you develop your potential. You can learn from whatever is at hand. Whatever you do, notice how you are; whatever you are experiencing, contact your feelings, thoughts, and the quality of your inner environment.

When you begin this practice, you will have to remind yourself to remain in touch with experience, and observation may have a strained quality. Try not to expect too much. Set aside a few minutes several times each day to ask simply, "What's happening?" Then, as observation becomes easier, ask yourself this question more frequently. In time a lively engagement between body, mind, and awareness will manifest in every activity. Eventually, observation becomes effortless, free of judgment, a gentle touch that does not disrupt the natural flow of the mind.

There are simple techniques that will help to stimulate this self-observation. For example, you can choose a word that you use many times each day—a word like *yes* or *hello*—and, for a day or two, substitute an alternative word. Watch your reactions carefully. Do you become frustrated and give up? Do you become tense when you slip and use the usual word? Does a lapse evoke thoughts such as, "I am a failure; I'll never amount to anything"?

Playful yet persistent self-observation, aided by such an exercise, can teach a great deal. You can begin to see how mind and body are connected: a change in one affects the other. Specific thoughts may be seen to be associated with particular bodily sensations and feelings. You might also recognize those circumstances that arouse emotions and cause you to behave in particular ways.

However, after you have discovered something important or gained a special insight, return to direct observation until there is nothing left to interpret or explain. Insights are like shiny rocks on the seashore: we want to pick them up and keep them. But we collect one, then another, and still more, until our load is so heavy we can hardly walk! Empty your pockets; let go of the insights that arise, no matter how valuable they seem, and open to a wider view, one that does not derive its meaning from any conceptual framework.

I f you uncover an unpleasant quality such as fear, hatred, or selfishness, do not avoid it or try to get rid of it. Pushing an emotion away is like throwing a rubber ball against a wall—the more energy you put behind it, the harder it returns. Clinging to a negative feeling will also ensure that it continues. For example, harboring the feeling that you are a bad person will perpetuate its harmful effect. Just acknowledge such negative energies in yourself and let them be, neither going toward them in fascination nor moving away from them out of fear. When judgments arise, note them but don't become involved in their content. Remain centered in your immediate experience, and you will eventually transcend these self-images that initially seem so negative.

Whenever you feel yourself being pulled off balance, or when agitation begins to arise, simply change your perspective. Imagine that your problems are above you, a tiny speck in the vast expanse of sky. Concentrate your consciousness on this point, even your awareness of yourself doing the exercise, and at the same time allow a knowing quality to spread in all directions beneath you, like the land and sky surrounding your point of consciousness. See if this exercise lightens the intensity of your difficulties. Gaining a wider perspective is like opening a window in a stuffy room—the whole atmosphere changes and the fresh breeze carries alternatives to our habitual ways of reacting.

Through the practice of self-observation in meditation and daily life, even our deepest questions can be answered. We can find out who we are and what we are doing on this earth. Ultimately, we may contact a body of knowledge so extensive that it touches everything.

Emotions and Balance

Just by sitting quietly and watching
our emotional state without
attachment, we become tranquil.

A natural, vibrant response to life—engendering enthusiasm, joy, and vitality—depends on inner balance. When we are balanced, positive qualities manifest spontaneously and we flow easily with whatever experience brings. But at times we lose our equilibrium and our perceptions become colored by emotion. The lucid and stimulating quality of happiness is clouded by anxiety and depression, and it is difficult to find fulfillment in anything we do.

If we suffer a serious physical injury, we are immediately advised to stay still, for moving about and becoming excited can make the injury worse. Similarly, in the midst of a problem, becoming emotional almost always makes it harder for us to find a solution. If we can stand back, however, and calmly observe every side of the situation, including the beginning of our emotional response, we will handle the problem more easily and also learn something of value for the future.

Nevertheless, until we have gained experience with our emotional patterns, it may be difficult to catch an emotion before it dictates our response to a situation. Thus at first we know our emotions only by their results—angry replies, tears, or longing for a loved one. Yet as we become more familiar with our patterns, we learn to recognize the early signs of an emotional reaction: a tight, physical sensation of excitement in the abdomen, which slowly spreads into the chest, causing a dense feeling in the heart or at times in the throat. Unless we can catch the energy at some point during this process, it will be followed almost immediately by an emotional response.

If we can relax before the sensation changes to emotion, the tension in our hearts can loosen. One method of becoming calm is simply to be mindful of the present moment, without becoming anxious about the future or preoccupied with the past. We can do this in any situation, just by *being* in that situation, allowing the experience to happen. But we must let go of expectations and concepts, or our emotions will gain control of our actions.

After an emotion has already surfaced, there are two ways to deal with it. One is to objectify the emotional response by blaming someone or something for the way you feel. This way reinforces and escalates negative feelings. The other choice is to go directly into the emotion, become it, discover it, feel it thoroughly, and calmly watch its nature. Rather than ask *why*, observe *how* the emotion arises. Instead of trying to push the emotion away, befriend it. If you watch carefully, without involvement, you will see this emotion manifest in both body and mind and then dissolve into pure energy.

Just by sitting quietly and watching our emotional state without attachment, we become tranquil. No other instruction is necessary. Agitated, restless feelings are like muddy water, which becomes still and transparently clear when left to stand. As our emotional reaction naturally subsides, mind and body become peaceful and balanced.

If we do not allow this change, we will see that we are holding the emotion fixed in the body, breath, and mind. Looking deeply into this emotional tension, we may discover a strange paradox: although we do not want to suffer, we seem unable to give up our unhappiness. We either cannot or will not change. We hold on to emotional responses, even the negative ones, because our emotional needs and attachments are very strong; they form a major part of our identity. Letting go of them can be very frightening and confusing, for without these familiar feelings we may no longer be sure who we are.

$\mathcal{W}$ orking with emotions can be difficult, and it is tempting to imagine that there is another place where problems don't exist. But *this* is your life—here and now. Once this moment's opportunity is gone, you can never get it back. If your precious energy is repeatedly spent on emotion and self-delusion, you will come to the end of life without realizing the deeper aspects of your experience. So whatever your situation and whatever your resources—body, mind, energy, awareness—use them fully right now, instead of wasting your time caught up in emotional turmoil.

The more you take responsibility for your feelings and emotions, and work with them—not just occasionally, but moment by moment, in all situations—the more balanced and healthy you will feel. Eventually, when an emotion arises it will last only a short time, and you will wake up almost immediately. You become like a dancer who has practiced for many years: although she may stumble and fall, she can regain her balance so quickly that every movement appears an integral part of the dance.

Sustaining Meditation

Know that however difficult experiences may be,
they are part of the truth you seek.

T he reasons for studying the Dharma, for following the path of meditation, are as different as the people who decide to travel the path. We may be motivated by the many benefits that can be derived from spiritual practice—good health, satisfying relationships, freedom, and happiness. The suffering of others provides another strong incentive to practice: if we become sensitive to their physical and mental pain, we may choose to follow a spiritual way of life in order to learn how to relieve this unhappiness.

There is still another reason, even more compelling than a desire for happiness or a wish to help others. Throughout history, people from all cultures have searched for meaning in their lives. This urge to learn and discover is the single most powerful motivation for taking the spiritual path, the path of self-knowledge.

When beginning this quest, we may simply ask questions and look closely at others to see what they know, to see if they have anything to offer that can help us make sense of things. Soon, however, we discover that this method of looking is limited. Others may give us helpful advice, but we can gain certainty only through our own experience, by a process of self-discovery.

Meditation provides the key for unlocking the secrets of our mind, as well as the means to relieve human suffering. This sounds wonderfully promising; the thought that our practice can bring understanding and happiness seems to provide all the inspiration we will ever need.

But when we have just begun to meditate, this kind of motivation has not been tested by any challenges. It is mostly an idea, and thus rather easy to maintain. After we meditate for a while, conflicts, doubts, and frustrations may arise; then our motivation must move to a deeper level, a level of action rather than mere intention.

Many people find that the initial stage of meditative practice intensifies previously concealed mental attitudes and traits. Resistance, anger, boredom, and other negative habit patterns come into awareness. When these feelings surface in meditation, we can be overwhelmed by anxiety and doubt about the actual benefits of practice. We may be bored, have trouble staying awake during meditation, or suddenly remember something else we have to do. We may not practice for weeks or even months. Though we recognize the value of meditation, we may come to feel that it is in conflict with other aspects of our life: for example, we might often have to choose between practice and entertainment or social contact. Perhaps the biggest obstacle to our progress is a sense that these conflicts make us ill-suited for the practice of meditation. If we take this feeling seriously, it can lead us to stop meditating altogether.

I t is a rare individual who does not encounter these and many other difficulties when beginning to practice—and it is especially important during these times to persevere. Read good books that can help you to understand your practice more deeply; encourage yourself to look at your life and meditation in fresh ways. Keep alive your purpose in practicing; know that however unpleasant or difficult these experiences may be, they are part of the truth you seek. Rather than closing your eyes and turning away from them, look more deeply and try to understand the truth unfolding in your life. Give yourself time and space to fully appreciate what is happening. Great calm and clarity may not appear instantaneously, or may last only a short time, but as long as you are patient and motivated to practice, these qualities will surely be realized.

Even after you have practiced for some time, and meditation comes more easily, you may find yourself feeling numb and dull, or bored with your practice. To transform this mood, meditate loosely, yet energetically. Allow your intelligence to guide you, and relax as much as possible, not getting too involved in evaluating your meditation or judging your experience.

When you are faced with conflicts, it may be helpful to talk to a teacher or an experienced friend. A good teacher knows you well and is able to make suggestions that are appropriate to you and your level of spiritual development. Because he has confronted similar experiences on his own path of growth, he can point the way. His understanding is sure and objective, and he can provide the necessary momentum when your motivation begins to falter.

A story is told of one of the Buddha's disciples who was a musician. After many apparently unsuccessful attempts at meditation, the disciple felt frustrated and asked the Buddha for instruction. "When you play beautiful music, do you play very *hard?*" the Buddha asked. "No," answered the musician, "that is not the way it is." "Well, then," continued the teacher, "do you play very *soft?*" "No," replied the disciple, "that is not it either. You must feel the right way to play, not too hard, not too soft. You must find the balance point that feels just right." "That is how to meditate," replied the Buddha.

At every stage of development, it is important to cultivate a balanced approach to practice. On the one hand, you need to encourage yourself, but you should also be alert to the possibility that the quality of your motivation will change. If you practice with dedication and patience, meditation will become an integral part of your life. Then you will no longer need to make an effort: meditation will arise naturally, like the morning sun.

Samsara and the Dharma

The transience of the things you most
cherish can inspire you to search for
something that cannot be taken from you.

I f we look honestly at our everyday lives, what do we see? All experience is impermanent. No matter what we do or think, in time we will age, losing our vitality and health; eventually we will die. We can no more change this than we can prevent the sun from shining or the seasons from following their age-old cycle. Yet it is difficult for us to accept this truth.

Moving restlessly from experience to experience, we seek pleasure and try to avoid suffering. But even while pleasant feelings are fresh, they are unstable. In every situation enjoyment is eventually followed by disappointment. Precious new possessions gradually lose their attraction; a relationship with a new love sours as we come to know the idiosyncracies of our partner. Even our children, for whom we hope so much, fail to meet our expectations.

We may seek wealth and success, hoping that they will solve our problems, and be drawn into projects, thoughts, and emotions that consume both time and energy. But our fantasies, however colorful, are seldom realized. Even if we make many sacrifices and reach our goals, something still seems lacking.

Eventually it becomes clear that our lives are not productive or beneficial for ourselves or the world. Like a dream animal, we run through a desert pursuing a mirage. The more we run, the hotter we become; the drier and more depleted our energy, the more vivid the mirage appears. Running itself intensifies our craving.

The drive for prosperity and achievement leads us astray because we are seeking answers in the wrong place. Looking to the future, pinning our hopes on beautiful dreams, we lose much of the value of our lives. We fall into patterns of needing and wanting, and lose the delicate inner balance that is our real source of nourishment and satisfaction.

There is really no way that we can 'fix' samsara, our ordinary existence, so that it becomes fully satisfying. As long as we are caught within it, we will be subject to its cycles of hope and fear, enjoyment and frustration, pleasure and pain. Sometimes we refuse to admit this. "Surely things will get better soon," we say to ourselves, putting off any attempt to bring about fundamental change. At other times we develop a pessimistic attitude: "I can't possibly change anything, so why bother to try?"

Indeed, it may seem hopeless, this samsaric existence. Where can we go that unhappiness does not follow like a shadow? Yet if we resign ourselves to disappointment, we will have lost a priceless opportunity.

The teachings of Buddhism, called the Dharma, tell us that to understand the hopelessness of samsara is to enter the path to nirvana, or liberation from suffering. This path carries us directly to the heart of samsara and teaches us to transform it into peace. When we follow the Dharma, our self-concepts, desires, and negative habits themselves provide the energy that fuels our spiritual growth. Every aspect of every situation becomes a process of training, learning, and understanding. The teachings become a silent song—a thread running through every moment—leading us to greater knowledge and awakening.

*T*herefore, encourage yourself to study the Dharma and realize its wisdom in your daily life. From the moment you wake up each day—and even during sleep—make every sensation and thought your spiritual practice. You can contact the teachings not only on the level of words and concepts, but internally, within daily experience. Your own frustration can push you toward a way to ease all pain and conflict. The impermanence of everything that matters to you, the transience of the relationships and things you most cherish can inspire you to search for something that cannot be shaken loose or taken from you. And when you have found this great power and direction through the teachings, you will no longer have to search for satisfaction: you will find all you need within your own heart.

You may still live in the same way, look the same, dress the same, but there will be a tremendous difference in your internal experience and in the way you relate to the world and to others. Feelings, sensations, and attitudes will grow smoother and more stable, giving rise to a sense of satisfaction and happiness, and a peaceful assurance that you are going in the right direction. Even when frightening or frustrating events develop, they will not disturb your inner balance and confidence. Within every experience you will see the truth of the Dharma. You may even come to see that samsara and nirvana are inseparable, like two sides of a coin, and that the journey from suffering to its cessation is not necessarily long and difficult. The moment you completely let go of samsara, nirvana is there.

The beauty within each thought and feeling is a source of security, protection, and strength. Our self-imposed limitations fall away before the limitless ability and intelligence of this deeper awareness. Within the space of our deeper mind, everything is perfect. Despite the apparent difficulties common to our lives, here the essence of consciousness is seen to be peace.

TWO

Deepening Awareness

Laziness

Laziness and vigor are innate
in all of us, and we can choose
which to foster in our everyday lives.

The laziness mind will speak intimately to you, advising you like a true friend. Whispering in your ear, beckoning you, it promises you enjoyment and satisfaction with no effort on your part. But this laziness mind never tells you that to get what it has to offer, you must give up everything of true and lasting value. All this is portrayed in the following story.

Lelo Sempa and Tsondru Nyidpa were brothers who lived in Tibet not so many years ago. When the time came to set out into the world to seek their fortune, they traveled together. Lelo, the elder, was a very good talker, and he was often able to get his way on the strength of this ability. Tsondru, though not as agile-minded as his brother, was strong and good-hearted, and willing to work hard to accomplish his goals.

As they traveled, the brothers often walked for many miles in silence. During these times Tsondru devised a strategy for accomplishing his goal: he would find work in a big city and save enough to buy his own store. Lelo, on the other hand, spent the hours of silence dreaming of the pleasant life he hoped for, a life filled with wealth, many comforts, and devoted friends. When he wasn't dreaming of the future, Lelo would walk for miles relishing memories of happy occasions in the past. When they shared their thoughts with each other, Tsondru would tell Lelo of his ambitions, and Lelo would offer Tsondru advice on how to realize his goals.

Tsondru had abundant enthusiasm and was always willing to do whatever needed to be done. When they made camp each night, it was Tsondru who gathered the wood for the fire and cooked the evening meal, while Lelo offered observations, such as "If you move the kindling closer together, the fire will grow hotter and our rice will cook faster." Lelo's recommendations were so useful that Tsondru did not notice that they were the only contributions Lelo ever made.

Lelo, for his part, did not overlook Tsondru's industrious and willing nature, and gradually he realized that an alliance with Tsondru could easily ensure the realization of his dreams for fortune and leisurely living. One day he suggested to Tsondru, "When we reach the city, my brother, let us join as partners in business; together we will surely be very successful." Tsondru considered this proposal as they walked, and at length he replied, "You are quick-witted and have much common sense; I think it would be a wise decision to work with you." And thus the partnership was sealed.

Finally the brothers came to Shigatse, a large Tibetan city filled with the commotion of people making their living. They decided to stay there, and Tsondru immediately began to think about work. "Come, Lelo," he urged, "let us find jobs so that we can save enough money to buy our own store." But Lelo replied that he needed time to get to know the city better, and to investigate all the possibilities before taking work. He pointed out that there was plenty of time, and that a smart man moved cautiously on such occasions. So Tsondru went out alone and soon found a job. His income was enough to support both of them, but left nothing for savings. Because Tsondru believed that Lelo, too, would soon find work, he happily provided for his brother.

ithin a short time, Lelo's quick wit and easy manner won him many friends. The small house that he shared with Tsondru was often filled with people. Beer flowed plentifully, and the conversation was always exciting. The lifestyle was pleasant and enjoyable, and Tsondru felt content; he hardly noticed that Lelo had altogether stopped looking for a job.

Tsondru worked well and, as a result, his employer gave him more responsibility. His income also increased, but after the expensive parties his brother arranged were paid for, there was still not enough to save. As months passed into years, Tsondru all but forgot his plan to buy his own shop.

Occasionally one of the brothers' friends would take Tsondru aside and politely point out that Lelo contributed little to their lives. "Will he ever find work?" the friend would ask. "What are his plans? It seems he does no more than pass his time in idle pleasures."

Such questions always left Tsondru feeling puzzled and anxious, yet he staunchly defended Lelo. "Lelo needs time to find a really good position," he would say. "And besides, we are always surrounded by congenial company; we never want for entertainment. So you see, he *does* make some contribution."

onetheless, doubt began to grow in Tsondru's mind, finally prompting him to go to his brother with a question. "Lelo, every so often one of our friends asks why you do not work. Can you tell me why you don't?"

Lelo thought for a moment and then replied, "Little brother, why do you listen to the words of others who do not have your best interests at heart? These people indulge in idle talk; perhaps they are jealous of our happy life. Maybe they wish to turn you against me. Whatever their motive, why encourage such pointless gossip? There are better things to do with your time, and better friends to be had. So put this question out of your mind, and go about your business."

Satisfied with this reply, Tsondru let the matter drop. But before long, Tsondru's employer ran upon hard times and was forced to close his business. Tsondru was out of a job, and, having been sent away at midday, went to think things over in the local tea shop. As he was sitting lost in thought, a young man approached and asked if he could share the table. Tsondru made room for the young man, and asked his name.

"I am Gewa Choskyi, and I have just arrived in Shigatse. I plan to find a job so that I can save enough money to buy a small business. Do you know of a good place to look for work in this city?"

The young man's eyes were bright, his character energetic and enthusiastic. It was easy to see that he would certainly accomplish his aims. His enthusiasm contrasted sharply with the dull emptiness that filled Tsondru's heart.

Then Tsondru realized that he had lost a very precious opportunity. Just like young Gewa, he had had great ambitions. He, too, had looked forward to having his own business, succeeding in his work, and realizing satisfaction and contentment from his efforts. But somehow things had not turned out like that. Here he was, no longer young, having lost his job; and except for memories of social occasions with his friends, he had very little to show for his life.

The more Tsondru pondered the matter, the more he realized that Lelo's influence lay at the heart of his emptiness. Lelo had promised to contribute much, but in truth had only taken from Tsondru; little by little he had eaten up Tsondru's energy and time, and undermined Tsondru's life plans.

Turning to Gewa, Tsondru said, "When I was your age, I too arrived in Shigatse, seeking my fortune. I had plans like yours, but they were never realized, because I was too willing to accept a life of comfort. Just today, I lost my job; my life is half over, and I have nothing saved. I want to advise you: I do not know where you can find work, but find it quickly, and work hard. Don't let others' words dissuade you from your goal. If they urge you to take more leisure time, or say that you work too hard, don't listen—they are not good friends.

Listen instead to your heart, your goal, and follow what it says. Then, when you are my age you will be more than content—your life will be full and rich, and your heart proud and confident. Even if you lose all the wealth you accumulate, you will still prosper, for you will possess the treasure of deep satisfaction and appreciation of your life." Gewa Choskyi quietly thanked Tsondru, and the older man left the teahouse.

The talk with Gewa Choskyi had helped Tsondru put his own life into perspective. It also helped him realize what he would do next. Arriving home, he found his brother surrounded by the usual group of friends. Tsondru said, "My friends, please leave us, for I must speak to my brother privately."

"But can't it wait, Tsondru? We are in the middle of a very good story and do not want to miss the end."

Tsondru shook his head and said "No," and from the tone of his voice everyone knew that it would be best to leave. Lelo moved uneasily to close the door behind their departing friends, saying, "What is it that must take precedence over our guests?"

Tsondru replied, "To begin with, Lelo, I lost my job today. We have no income now. While I was thinking of what to do next, I realized that this life we have created has really given us nothing. I also realized that I am growing old and have done little to accomplish my goals in life. But I am not yet too old to pursue them, so I have decided to leave you, travel to another city, and begin again. I am determined to realize my aims. Before I leave, I must also say that you too should stop wasting your life. Your tongue is agile and has won you many friends, but it has provided you with little else. You are older than I am, yet you are dependent on me for your support—what will you do after I have gone?"

For once, Lelo had no ready answer. He pleaded with Tsondru to change his mind and stay, but Tsondru did not respond. Lelo then became angry and accused Tsondru of betraying him, of leaving him to pursue selfish aims. Next he accused Tsondru's employer of forcing him into this rash decision. Lelo placed blame on everything and everyone that came to mind, but would not consider his own laziness as the source of the problem.

Tsondru left and settled in another city. Within two years he had saved enough to buy the business he had dreamed of, and he soon became prosperous and well-regarded. Tsondru's brother Lelo, however, spent the rest of his life wandering from town to town, telling stories in the local taverns in exchange for food and companionship.

I n Tibetan, the word *lelo* means laziness, and *tsondru* means vigor. Both qualities are innate in all of us, and we can choose which of these qualities to foster in our everyday lives.

The laziness mind pretends to be a friend to us, offering us comfort and enjoyment, but in truth it slowly consumes our most cherished dreams, and weighs us down so that we can barely move. It is the biggest obstacle to our progress on the spiritual path. When we set out to practice each day, the laziness mind tells us to wait, rest awhile, or do something else, for there will be time for practice later. This mind always seems sensible, and, like Tsondru, we can be hypnotized by its "lazy logic."

But we can turn away from laziness, and listen instead to the wisdom of our inner nature. By developing strength and vigor, and by pursuing our goals with patience, we can withstand the seductions of *lelo*. We can provide ourselves with the confidence that comes from using our energies in a fruitful way. Once we break free from the laziness mind, there is no limit to what we can do.

The Power of Breath

*While the outer breath brings
nourishment to the body,
the inner breath carries the
vital quality of enlightenment
to our whole being.*

The breath can be a powerful ally on the spiritual path, carrying knowledge, awareness, and nourishment throughout our body and mind. We live within the rhythm of breath, and by becoming attuned to its patterns, we find an avenue that leads directly to our inner nature.

To appreciate the power and potential of breath, we must distinguish two types of breathing. The first is the outer breath, our physical respiration. As meditation practice develops, this breath grows soft and still, allowing us to recognize a second, more subtle breath. Smooth, silent, and full of feeling, this inner breath circulates throughout our entire being.

The inner breath effects powerful changes through its relation to the energy centers of the body.* When energy

*See Tarthang Tulku, *Kum Nye Relaxation*, Part 1 (Berkeley, California: Dharma Publishing, 1978), pp. 36–39.

flows well through these centers, we are in good health, both mentally and physically. The energy of the subtle breath restores balance, relieving tension and blockages while increasing the integration of body and mind.

Although the inner breath is a potent means of transformation, contacting it may be difficult at times. When we are excited or upset, our outer breath becomes rapid and heavy, and we cannot touch the subtle feelings within. Then it can be frustrating to try to breathe fully and deeply. This frustration, in turn, can stir up emotions and fill the mind with images and concepts which lead us to become even more unbalanced.

Purposeless talking also prevents contact with our inner breath. As we engage in such talk, thoughts and emotions are stirred up; we agree and disagree, forming opinions and perhaps falling into arguments or negativity. These patterns of speculation and emotion sap the vitality of our inner breath, and leave us feeling drained.

To develop awareness of the subtle breath, practice simple attention to your physical respiration. Notice when your breathing is slow and when it is fast. Cultivate a slow, steady rhythm; such even breathing in times of stress will stimulate a nourishing flow of inner breath. Be mindful, too, of how this gentle breathing affects your speech. Once you have developed an appreciation of inner breath, you will naturally speak less and with more meaning.

As our meditation deepens, the inner breath grows stronger and more pervasive. In deep meditation outer breathing becomes completely still, and only the smooth inner breath continues to function. Aware and light, this inner breath carries the vital quality of enlightenment to our whole being.

V isualization practices can also stimulate the smooth flow of the subtle breath. One example of such a practice is silent chanting of the mantra OM AH HUM. As you inhale, inwardly chant OM while visualizing all knowledge being drawn into your body and mind. The entire universe gathers within the field of OM.

For the moment that the breath is retained in the body, silently say AH. This syllable transforms the energy of the universe into a still and open realm. Then, as you exhale, silently chant HUM. With HUM the enlightened energy flows back into the universe, to spread its benefits in all directions. In this way, repeat OM AH HUM silently with each breath. Sometimes you can concentrate on the syllables, sometimes on the meaning, or on the feeling of the breath itself. Eventually these three will merge, and the practice will no longer be a reminder of our enlightenment nature, but an expression of enlightenment itself.

Try to practice this visualization as much as you can during the day; the more you do it, the greater the benefits will be. Wherever you are and no matter what you are doing, you can do this simple practice. Instead of distracting you, it will increase your awareness of the present moment. It can be especially effective when you are tense or agitated. Taking a few moments to breathe OM AH HUM will free the inner breath to soothe your tensions with its stimulating warmth

As you grow more sensitive to the flow of the subtle breath, its pervasive whisper will communicate with your mind and heart, guiding you to relaxation and deep clarity. All of your experience will glow with a vibrant quality, and you will discover a powerful calm that can extend to everyone around you, encouraging harmony and joy. This infinite peace and clarity is always available: you can touch it in your very next breath.

Healing through Mantra

Mantra is like a wish-fulfilling gem that
awakens the subtle energy of the enlightened mind.

For many centuries mantras have been used in spiritual practice to focus and transform subtle energies. The practice of mantra enables us to restore a natural balance and harmony in our lives and to arrive at a quality of awareness that leads directly to the realization of enlightenment.

How do mantras work? Sound has a potent effect on our body and mind. It can soothe and please us, or have a disharmonious influence, producing a subtle feeling of irritation. Mantra is even more powerful than common sound: it is like a door that opens upon the depths of experience.

Since mantras have no conceptual meaning, they do not evoke predetermined responses. When we chant a mantra, we are free to transcend habitual reflexes. The sound of mantra can still the mind and senses, relax the body, and connect us with a natural healing energy.

The healing energies awakened by the sound of mantra are inherent in the psyche. In the Buddhist tradition these positive forces are characterized as deities: each deity embodies a teaching, a quality of experience that is integral to enlightenment. The deities evoked by the mantra are not some type of personality, but manifestations of a natural bliss and transformative power that lies within body, breath, and mind.

The following mantras are especially effective for healing specific problems and nurturing our inner awareness.

Tad Yatha Om Muni Muni Maha Muni Shakyamuni Ye Soha

The mantra of Shakyamuni Buddha transforms delusion and aids in self-healing. Visualizing or thinking of the Buddha while chanting can help release the mantra's beneficial power. This mantra is especially effective when chanted on the new moon and full moon days of each month.

Om Amitabha Hri

The mantra of Amitabha, Buddha of the Western direction, inspires clarity and compassion.

Om Mani Padme Hum Hri

This mantra transforms negative emotions and suffering through the limitless compassion of Avalokiteshvara. Like a sweet golden nectar, the sound of the mantra will ease the body and mind.

Om Ah Ra Pa Tsa Na Dhi

This is the mantra of Manjushri; it embodies all wisdom. Sparkling with the light of clear vision, the sword of Manjushri cuts through delusion and ignorance.

Om Ah Hum Vajra Guru Padma Siddhi Hum

Guru Padmasambhava's mantra, an antidote for confusion and frustration, has a particularly powerful transformative effect in this age of turmoil. It is most effective when chanted very early in the morning.

Mantra practice is especially valuable to us today because it is simple and direct. All we need to do is relax as much as possible while rhythmically repeating the syllables of the mantra, either silently or aloud. If this is done with an open attitude and with confidence in the power of the mantra, chanting for just five to fifteen minutes a day will have a healing effect on the body and mind.

The more you repeat a mantra, or maintain awareness of it, the more its power is activated. The special energy of the mantras given above is traditionally evoked through one hundred thousand or more repetitions over a period of months or years. When enough of the healing energy of the mantra has accumulated, it can be directed toward positive ends, such as curing illness. In Tibet mantras were commonly used for healing, most often in conjunction with other medical treatment, although there have been instances of people curing themselves of potentially fatal diseases through the use of mantra alone.

Even more important than the capability of mantra to heal the body is its power to heal the mind. Mantra can help us maintain awareness during our daily activities. When we are distracted by the demands of family, job, and personal pursuits, when we lose a sense of equilibrium and groundedness, mantra can remind us to keep our mind concentrated and attuned to the flow of experience. Chanting silently or aloud throughout the day creates a balanced perspective that readily dissolves confusion and uncertainty. Mantra also gently opens and transforms emotional states, helping us to deal with any situation clearly and directly.

All Dharma, or teaching, can be interpreted through mantra. It is said that when Shakyamuni Buddha taught, he uttered only the one syllable Aн. From this syllable every listener understood the teachings perfectly in his own language, and in the manner most suitable for him. Through the power of mantra, all sounds gather into the enlightened field. The Sanskrit word *man* denotes the seed of the mind; *tra* means magical transmutation. Thus, mantra is like a wish-fulfilling gem that awakens the subtle energy of the liberated mind.

Thought

When you penetrate thought patterns,
the fixed quality of thought dissolves
into clarity and deep satisfaction.

For just five minutes, count your thoughts and see how many ideas and images arise. Day and night, one thought leads to another: our consciousness is preoccupied with images. Like flames leaping and flickering, thoughts jump into awareness and quickly consume our energy. We may imagine that we are solving problems, or creating new ideas and plans, but most often the mind is merely talking to itself, escaping into daydreams, wasting precious time.

As long as thought vibrations continue to play in this way, our consciousness will remain frozen in fixed views and automatic responses. When a word is spoken, an image is instantly projected in the mind, but *within* the image lies a deeper experience. By staying in the immediate moment, it is possible to enter the fluid realm of being that is the space within our thoughts.

When our involvement in images and concepts lessens, we can discover a quality of being that has no form and no specific characteristics. It has no position and no fixed view to defend. There is only a peaceful, light quality—a very healthy quiet that is the source of all life energy and creative activity. Memories of the past and projections of the future no longer occupy our attention. In the present moment, there is natural, unobstructed awareness.

Through meditation practice we can cultivate this awareness and contact the vast calm that underlies and pervades our thoughts. There are several ways to do this. One is to empty the mind of all concepts and images, so that only peace and clarity remain. But when dozens of thoughts can arise in only five minutes, quieting them all might take many years.

There is another way that is much quicker, and which can even bring immediate results if done correctly. We can learn to go directly into thoughts and crack them wide open, until thought itself becomes meditation. Instead of resisting a thought as it arises, step back a bit and relax, allowing the thought to be whatever it will. Watching very carefully, look for the subtle feelings that begin to emerge as the thought provokes a response, a judgment, or an evaluation. Try to catch the tendency of the mind to elaborate these feelings into more concepts, which further crystallize the experience.

When you penetrate thought patterns, the fixed quality of thought dissolves into clarity and deep satisfaction. This lucidity is complete awareness, needing no support or direction. Within its fullness you are not trying to *do* anything, you are no longer even trying to meditate. There is no 'thing' left to direct. You are the center of the thought, and the center is true balance.

There is no being, no subject-object relationship—these categories no longer exist. Yet far from being in a vacant, thoughtless state, you are exceptionally alert and responsive. Now the meditation truly comes alive. You simply sit and become your thoughts, fully in the present moment, without trying, without expectations, but with feeling. Thought itself becomes meditation and is no longer 'thought' as we normally experience it, because there is nothing left to hold on to.

Working with thoughts by opening them as they arise can bring many pleasant feelings, which—without attachment—also become our meditation. Then we begin to develop a larger mind. Thoughts come, or they don't, and it does not matter so much, for they no longer have the power to hypnotize and hold our awareness. We can go into each thought skillfully. We can even go into the thoughts that judge other thoughts, and, embracing this judging mind, become united with it.

When your mind is turbulent, or you are depressed, remember that the darker the negative side, the brighter the positive will be, and that the line dividing them can be crossed easily. Even in the worst possible situation, the light of liberation can shine within a single thought. You can find the enlightened heart of any moment.

By relying on the light of awareness you can see that the difficulties you face are manifestations of your own concepts. Going deeply into your thoughts, you will see how you create your experience, how you alone are the judge who determines heaven and hell, good and bad.

Where is the 'problem'? It does not have any independent existence outside your mind.

When you realize this, nothing can impede you. Whatever experience arises, stay with it, expand it, and heat it up. If you remain within the intense core of the experience, the meditator unites with thoughts and emotions, and everything dissolves. Then awareness grows powerful and one-pointed. As thoughts and emotions are increasingly included within this field of awareness, they become more useful. Instead of being a cause of frustration or confusion, they become agents of well-being, raw material for a healthy, virtuous mind.

The beauty within each thought and feeling is a source of security, protection, and strength. Our self-imposed limitations fall away before the limitless ability and intelligence of this deeper awareness. Within the space of our deeper mind, everything is perfect. Despite the apparent difficulties common to our lives, here the essence of consciousness is seen to be peace.

Patience

The balanced energy of patience
radiates a friendly and productive attitude
from our hearts into every aspect
of our existence.

Like spice in food, patience is the secret ingredient that makes life rich and fulfilling. Relaxed and allowing, this gentle friend gives us the time to appreciate experience, to deepen our involvement in all that we do. With patience we can face the future with assurance because, in the present, our senses are nourished and satisfied. Even when obstacles cast a shadow on our path, we know they can eventually be overcome through patience.

Without patience our lives are like trying to till a field with no horse to pull the plow—the furrows are shallow and crooked, the work is hard, and we become frustrated. But with the strong, steady help of patience, we can plow furrows that are straight and deep, and reap a rich harvest from our efforts. Our experience flows smoothly, and all our activities are purposeful.

Nowadays we seldom associate this idea of strength and reliability with patience. We may even consider patience a sign of passivity, weakness, or lack of intelligence. Because patience can appear slow or indirect to us, we may overlook its value, choosing instead an easier or faster course of action. Technology has quickened the pace of our lives, and impressed us with the idea that all tasks can be accomplished, all problems solved, with little or no exertion.

In our impatience we are like spoiled children who believe they will always get what they want when they want it. When we meet with obstacles or problems that cannot be readily overcome or quickly solved, we are surprised and easily defeated. As conflicts arise, we often become lost in escape fantasies, instead of looking honestly at our situation and taking decisive action to change it. Before long, our unresolved problems are like insects annoying us to the point of deep aggravation.

Impatience has a rough and heavy quality that debilitates both body and mind. When we impatiently pursue a goal, our breathing is rapid and sharp, our movements are erratic, and our thoughts run out of control. Rushing here and there, we can make frequent mistakes. Finally, if we do not accomplish what we set out to do, we become burdened by anxiety and discouragement.

In this way our potential for intelligent, positive action is held in check. We find ourselves under the sway of self-doubt, for ultimately impatience leaves us without support. Like a traitor to our efforts, impatience can persuade us to give up just as we near our goal. When this pattern of incompletion is repeated again and again, we grow increasingly self-critical and come to believe that everything we do will end in failure. This is the worst consequence of impatience, because once we lose hope, even the spiritual path cannot lead us anywhere. We can no longer appreciate the purpose of our practice; we have lost confidence in the value of our goal.

Patience is the best antidote for these difficulties. With its soft and accommodating energy, we can accept and work with our experience, rather than struggle against it. Then all our experience, whether positive or negative, can be appreciated. Yet ironically, even when we recognize the need to develop patience, we may be too impatient to do so. Instead of cultivating patience, we fight our impatience each time it appears. If we see ourselves becoming anxious, we try to force ourselves to calm down.

But impatience and anxiety can be our most valuable teachers of the practice of patience. Listen carefully to anxiety, for it can be a valuable sign that you need to relax and loosen your expectations and demands upon yourself. Learn to recognize how impatience arises. Watch the constriction of your mental and physical energy, the sense of urgency imparted to your thoughts and actions; note how impatience encourages the view that life is hopeless.

Instead of running after patience, relax and let it come to you. Loosen the tension in your body; open your concentration and allow your emotional energy to flow. Let the warm, soothing energy of patience arise within you and flow through your body easily and freely. This practice *is* the act of patience.

When you feel yourself becoming impatient, you can retreat to a cooler location, perhaps going for a walk in a high place where the air is clear. This environment can help you cultivate a peaceful and beautiful atmosphere within yourself.

Another way to transform impatience, anxiety, and emotion is to practice with colors. Pick a color that you like, and let yourself enjoy its qualities. Then bring the color to your internal awareness and allow it to touch and heal the impatience you are feeling. You can extend this exercise by concentrating on flowers, art, or other beautiful objects or images. Invite them into your awareness and feel their harmony and grace. Then let their forms transform the fragmented quality of impatience into the likable and smooth energy of patience.

Through patience, difficulties can be used to our advantage. Patience is like a best friend; it is comfortable to be with, open-minded and allowing. We may be moody, changeable, or overly critical, but patience accepts these qualities and cares for us on a deeper level. The balanced energy of patience moves easily throughout the body, radiating a friendly and productive attitude from our hearts into our work, our relationships, and every aspect of our existence.

Self-Images

When you look at the image directly,
it disperses—it is empty, insubstantial.

I f we observe the way we live from day to day, we find that much of our time is spent reinforcing fantasies of who we are and how we want others to see us. We are quite involved with our *self-images*. Watching these images, we can discern our characteristic ways of acting: the way we sit, the way we look, or the way we habitually talk.

Our self-images exert a strong influence on our lives, for they provide definitions, however inaccurate, for who we are. If we were somehow to divest ourselves of them, we might feel uncertain of our identity. Consequently we allow these images to perpetuate themselves until our capacity for spontaneous action is greatly reduced. Even when a situation invites a new response, we may hesitate to make it, because the momentum of thought and emotion tends to draw us into one pattern of behavior. Thus, our sense of freedom is diminished.

Hard and narrow like a yak's horn, self-images restrict our growth and deny us fulfillment and satisfaction.

A Tibetan children's story tells of a hungry bear that liked to hunt for groundhogs hibernating underground in winter. The bear dug around, found a groundhog, knocked it unconscious, and—thinking he had killed it—set it aside to eat later. But the groundhog woke up and ran away. Unaware of this, the bear dug up another groundhog, hit it hard, and set it aside. Then the bear wanted *more.* He looked around for a third groundhog, but in the meantime, the second one woke up and ran away. This pattern repeated itself over and over, until at the end the bear was left with nothing but the groundhog he held in his paws.

Like the bear, we attempt to feed our self-images without ever being fully satisfied. As energy is directed to fulfilling expectations, we are left unsupported, out of touch with our inner nature. Eventually, this approach to experience leaves us with little more to show for our efforts than memories of the past and dreams of the future.

But are self-images the only source of our dissatisfaction? Aren't there some *real* problems that are at least partially responsible for our discontent? Say, for example, we don't have a nice house, or a job, or enough money. Perhaps we are not liked by others, or are not beautiful. It is appealing to attribute our difficulties to outside causes; nevertheless, if we look deeply, we can see that we are unhappy because we are allowing our self-images to run our lives. Once we understand this, we can truly do something about our problems.

H ow can we lessen our involvement with our self-images and learn to become more flexible and open to experience? First we need to recognize these fantasies for what they are: images projected by the mind that have no reality in themselves. Why listen to what they are telling us? But it may be difficult at first to stop 'listening' to thoughts and emotions that are so much a habit we may not see them clearly. It is as if we have a close friend whose advice we've been following for many years. Suddenly we are told that he has been lying to us all this time. In order to be convinced, we need to examine our friend's words and decide for ourselves.

So it is with our self-images. By examining them carefully, we can learn to understand their true worth. One way to do this is to look directly at a self-image during a strong emotional upset. As the emotions take shape, intensify them, letting them build up until they become very strong and powerful. Make them so vivid and alive you can almost see and touch them. Feel them as fully as you can. Then use this vital energy to arouse your awareness to separate you from your image-making: step back and look directly at the situation you have created. What do you see?

When you look at the image directly, it disperses, for it is empty, insubstantial. True, the feeling is there, but as soon as you have lost interest in sustaining the image of yourself, in feeding it energy, its holding power dissolves.

You can also loosen your attachment to a self-image by changing moods in a skillful way. To begin, go into the unhappiness you feel; embrace it totally, without res-

ervation or judgment. Then suddenly leap to the positive side of the experience: *be happy*. Even if you do not
feel happy at first, strongly remind yourself that you are
happy until you can relax in the open and light aspects
of the experience. How is the positive side? Look at the
differences between the positive and negative qualities.

When you can see both sides, you can choose either
to develop the self-image which restricts you, or to foster
the positive side, which offers fulfillment and liberation.
When you are dominated by the image, you are neither
independent nor liberated; there is no real sense of com-
pleteness. You feel pressured, under the control of some
unidentifiable agent. The light side, however, is balanced
and fulfilling. Instead of desiring something or feeling
restless to go somewhere, you nourish yourself directly.
You feel complete just as you are.

Through practice of this exercise with different self-
images, your mind will become more flexible, and
you will develop a deep acceptance of your experience.
This acceptance is not the kind that requires a forceful act
of will, as when we say to ourselves, "I need to accept
this." Instead, it is an effortless opening to whatever is
happening.

When you can easily jump from the negative side of
your experience to the positive, you may find that you
can almost feel both at the same time—somewhat like
looking into a mirror and being equally aware of your
body and its reflection at the same moment. Then you
may see that there *is* no jumping from one quality to
another; there actually is only awareness itself, both
within and around experience.

Complete satisfaction in life is possible for all of us. But to realize this satisfaction we must choose a balanced approach to our experience. In every situation we have the choice of which way we would like to go. By choosing the side of light and freedom, we are assured of ever-increasing fulfillment and purpose in life.

Love and Compassion

When you have gone beyond giver and
gift and recipient, you have reached compassion.

Everyone feels a need for contact and support, and it is natural to think that the fulfillment of this need will come from relationships with others. Most of us are taught that love is outside us, something to be obtained. Thus when we do find it, we hold it tightly to ourselves, as if there were not enough to go around. But as love becomes selfish grasping, we cut ourselves off from true intimacy.

The most rewarding love we can realize is the love that is already within us, at the heart of our being. Here there is an infinite source of warmth that we can use to transform our loneliness and unhappiness. As we contact this nurturing energy, we find the inner resources necessary to be truly responsible for our own growth and well-being. We learn to maintain a healthy body and mind, and to care for ourselves in the best possible way in every situation. When our ability to fulfill our own genuine needs expands, we are able to truly help others as well.

If you feel that love is missing from your life, you can create the positive warmth of love within your heart. Let yourself feel this inner glow; expand it, letting it touch all your experience with a gentle happiness. The more you do this, the more love you discover within, and the more you have to offer others. You can become truly self-sufficient, not needing to rely on family, friends, or lovers. No longer must your relationships be based on insecurity or emptiness; you can be free to express your feelings fully, and to deeply appreciate yourself and those around you.

As you develop the ability to contact this caring within your heart, you can use its energies to maintain balance in your life. Whenever you feel depressed or hopeless, use love to transform these feelings. If you find yourself going to the other extreme of excitement and exhilaration, do not let yourself be carried away, but find a stable peace in the warmth within. The more you nurture yourself in this way, the stronger your self-confidence will be; you will develop a certainty as indestructible as a diamond. You will find within yourself your own best protector and friend.

As love grows within you, make a gift of it. Start by offering yourself complete acceptance, then share this love with all other beings. Feel this love for others deeply, especially for those who are ignorant, dissatisfied, or deluded. Offer your love unreservedly, without prejudice, even to those who seem cruel or who have done harm to you or others. Share your love with all who have mental or physical pain; even if you cannot offer concrete help, you can *feel* that you are giving to them, helping them, making them happy. As you open your heart in this way, you will find that your love kindles a warmth in the hearts of those around you, and gradually spreads to touch the lives of all beings.

In this way, by learning to be kind to ourselves, and responding to the suffering of others, we begin to develop a compassionate attitude. But until we have passed beyond all dualistic notions, *compassion* has limited scope. Our serving, helping, and concern is a gesture toward compassion, a movement toward complete openness, but it is not yet a fully realized expression.

What seems to be purely compassionate may really be somewhat self-oriented, based on grasping. We like certain feelings and responses, so we tend to act in a way that stimulates them. We may think that we are giving without expectations or demands when we are actually partly motivated by emotional hunger. Even experienced meditators may have traces of this grasping. Only as we let go of it can compassion arise.

To develop true compassion, cultivate open awareness in your meditation. Work to stimulate positive feelings and transcend self-images, with their expectations and demands. The more open you become, the more you will be able to offer assistance to all living beings. And the more you respond to the problems of others, the more your own problems will dissolve. Gradually, the distinction between your welfare and the welfare of others disappears, and you see that when you are no longer self-preoccupied, there is no individual problem. When you have gone beyond achieving, beyond thoughts, beyond giver and gift and recipient, beyond all dualities, then you have reached compassion. When giving is completely free of attachment and grasping, it is significant and appropriate, the natural expression of an awakened heart.

Compassion is open, free, and limitless. Indescribable and utterly beyond intellectual comprehension, it responds to any situation spontaneously and without calculation, yet in a way that enlightens and transforms. Indeed, compassion may be compared to sunlight, since it awakens and brings joy to beings; compassion is also like a rainbow, its ineffable beauty lifting the hearts of all who see it.

Though we may not yet be capable of showing true compassion, contemplating its immeasurable depth may help put our problems into perspective. Even the thought that each of us is capable of becoming compassionate, or of becoming compassion itself, can have a highly beneficial effect. As we seek to implement the teachings of the Buddha in our daily lives, learning to deal with everyday situations in a practical and positive way, this vision of the final goal can inspire us with a feeling of unlimited beauty and joy.

The surest refuge in the world is the freedom of our being. Once we are in touch with natural being, we live free from resistance, responsive to all aspects of experience. We participate fully in life, understanding and fulfilling our unique opportunity as human beings.

THREE

Participation

Surrendering
to the Teachings

*Surrendering to the teachings is
the giving up of self-images,
fears, thoughts, and desires into
the hands of deeper self-knowledge.*

The Buddha once told his cousin that he should study and practice Dharma more, but his cousin refused, saying, "I have no time. I am in love with a beautiful woman and can't leave her. Besides, I don't enjoy studying."

The Buddha then asked, "Would you like to come with me to a different land?" His cousin said yes, and, taking hold of the Buddha's robe, was at once lifted to a heavenly realm. Soon after their arrival, the Buddha said that he wished to meditate and walked off, leaving his cousin alone. The young man looked around in amazement, finding radiance and beauty everywhere. Men and women were listening to teachings, walking in the gardens, and dancing. Angelic beings flew joyfully through the air.

The Buddha's cousin soon noticed, however, that while everyone else was enjoying the companionship of others, he was alone. He wished that he, too, could participate. He came to a magnificent palace and entered, hoping to find someone to talk to. Inside were four incomparably beautiful women, with whom he struck up a conversation. "Who lives in this palace?" he asked.

"Oh, we are the only occupants now," they replied. "But a certain man who is becoming interested in practicing the Dharma will eventually be reborn here, because he is creating positive karma. We are waiting for him."

"Who is this lucky man?" he asked. The women replied that he was the Buddha's cousin. Elated by their answer, the young man immediately returned to the Buddha and asked permission to become a student. The Buddha accepted him and took him back to the worldly realm to study the Dharma.

This cousin was Nanda, one of the Buddha's closest disciples. In the beginning Nanda was attracted to the Dharma because he wanted to live with the women he met in the heavens. The Dharma and its practices did not seem important; his only thought was to gain more pleasure and happiness. However, Nanda persevered in his studies and later became an Arhat, renouncing everything. Then when he was asked about the heavenly realm, he replied, "Forgotten." Realizing the Dharma, he found he did not need anything else.

Like Nanda, we are attracted by the Dharma because it appears to offer us what we think we need to be happy. But as we become more aware, we may see that our ideas of happiness are projections that the mind has grasped and substituted for real satisfaction and learning. The Dharma is not something that we can possess. Even though at first it seems to come to us from the outside— from a book, from our teacher, or from friends—the true Dharma arises from within; it flows in our blood and unites with our heart and mind.

If we think of the teachings as external and the practice as something added to our lives, we may study and practice for a long time without going beyond certain levels of attainment. Milarepa discussed this problem and its solution: "External feelings create the need for interpretations and block the way to absolute realization. So forget all relative truths and look within yourself. Forget all ideas, for they will not help you."

In our practice we learn to see in a wholly new way, not just to substitute one set of interpretations, one ordinary way of looking, for another. Replacing a worldly view with a spiritual view, or an American view with a Tibetan view changes only the external circumstances of our lives. It is important to go further than this, to transcend our perceptions altogether—and the easiest way to do this is through complete surrender to the Dharma.

The idea of surrendering usually means to give in, to passively submit to the control of someone or something stronger. To surrender to the Dharma, however, requires the active and continuously renewed commitment of our energy. Surrendering to the teaching is the giving up of our self-images, fears, thoughts, and desires into the hands of deeper self-knowledge. It is submitting to the control of our true nature, which is healthier and stronger than our surface experience can ever be.

Before we begin to trust in this way, we are like travellers who have been drifting around a foreign country for a long time. But when we surrender to the Dharma, we can relax and feel confident, because the Dharma is like a guide who can take us where we need to go. Even when we stumble on the painful awakenings that accompany the process of self-development, we can rely on our guide to support and protect us.

If we have faith in the Dharma, and follow the teachings with concentration and devotion, we will certainly realize the joy and deep satisfaction of complete fulfillment. The energy of enlightenment resides in our heart, guiding us and providing us with the inner light of our true nature. Surrendering to this higher energy is the perfect practice.

Natural Being

Everything precious, true, and beautiful
is within natural being.

atural being is our enlightened nature. This being is not something apart from us that we must recapture; we *are* this being. When we make natural being our spiritual home, truth and beauty arise as spontaneous gifts. Perfect knowledge shines into our lives, and our body, mind, and senses lead us effortlessly toward enlightenment. The spiritual path is as close as our heartbeat and breath.

Although the perfect harmony and ease of natural being are so near, they are often somehow elusive. We frequently have the anxious feeling that we lack something essential to our well-being. We may imagine fulfillment to lie in an ideal existence far away from our normal one, and tire ourselves out seeking for it.

Even by attempting to mold our meditation practice into a perfect pattern we can develop habits that keep us from accomplishing our aims. "Oh, this is not the right way to meditate," we say to ourselves. We think we are not getting anywhere, and criticize ourselves for lack of progress. But these judgments set up a boundary between us and meditation, and we lose touch with the flowing harmony of our nature. This situation is like being hungry and having nourishing food in the cupboard, but not eating it.

So rather than trying to identify wisdom, awareness, or meditation, rather than worrying about whether your meditation is good or bad, simply acknowledge these thoughts without getting caught up in their meaning. Don't give them power over you. Then there is no need to run away or hide from them—you don't need to *do* anything.

With no subject reaching out and no object to possess, being opens from within. Then you may say, "I can see a subtle difference from my usual experience. I'm excited at this discovery. I want to report it to myself." But the moment you try to express this experience or make it fit a conceptual model, it is gone. Although such reporting is an attempt to own and preserve the experience, it actually only separates you once again from natural being.

When such thoughts arise, or when we are experiencing a strong feeling or emotion, we can relax the interpretive side, the side which says, "This means something to me." Rather than becoming involved with interpretations, images, feelings, or sensations, we can remain with the energy in its pure form. Contacting the energy in this way, we may see that it touches the wholeness of being, like a raindrop falling into the ocean. Then we have found the way to convert our thoughts and emotions into meditative experience, opening the mind to the play of being.

$\mathcal{T}$ he more we participate in natural being, the less we need special techniques and the less we worry about finding answers to our questions. The wider our concept of the mind becomes, the more experience we can accept without making judgments. This acceptance itself becomes meditation, and we realize that meditation is an integral part of our experience. Everything precious, true, and beautiful is within natural being, so there is no need to look for special experiences or flashes of insight, or to report to the mind on what has happened. When we are in touch with our inner nature, the distinction between meditative and nonmeditative states dissolves.

Becoming attuned to natural being in this way makes life truly interesting. Dullness and boredom no longer arise. Whatever we see, hear, taste, or feel—whatever comes to us in life—becomes rich and alive. Life is interesting because, whether or not we succeed fully in what we intend, we always enjoy and appreciate our efforts.

A joyful, balanced way of living is our natural response to being. Our hearts open to others. Honesty and appreciativeness become our essential morality, and we do not complicate our life situations by insincerity or manipulation. We no longer create negative patterns, so further problems will not arise in the future. In this way, we move gradually toward enlightenment.

The surest refuge in the world is the freedom of our being. Once we are in touch with natural being, we live free from resistance, responsive to all aspects of experience. We participate fully in life, understanding and fulfilling our unique opportunity as human beings.

Teacher and Student

*Between teacher and student a bond is formed
that can never be broken—only transformed
by the realization of enlightenment.*

he biographies of the greatest masters of Buddhism
are filled with beautiful stories describing the cru-
cial role that teachers played in their training. Deep love
and appreciation shine forth in the descriptions of how
they met their teachers, the trials they faced, the teachings they received, and the realization they gained. The
teacher-student relationship is revealed to be as close
as that between parent and child: the guru tries to relieve the student's troubles and guide him away from
difficulties.

A relationship this close, and with such far-reaching
consequences, is not undertaken lightly. Ashvaghosha,
an important early Buddhist poet, wrote: "So that the
commitment between the teacher and student will not be
broken, there must be mutual examination beforehand
to determine whether each can brave a guru-disciple
relationship." Before a student chooses a teacher, he

must be sure that the teacher is qualified, capable, and compassionate. It is also important that the student feel respect and a sense of empathy toward the teacher. Once the student has made his choice, the teacher will test the student's determination and ability to pursue the spiritual path. Only when mutual trust is established does the teacher formally accept the student. When teacher and student have made their commitments to one another in this way, a bond is formed that can never be broken—only transformed by the realization of enlightenment.

By accepting a student, the teacher promises to work wholeheartedly for the well-being of the student, doing everything in his power to ensure the student's physical, mental, and spiritual health. Because of the teacher's wider experience and learning, he has greater responsibility to the student than the student has toward him. Recognizing the depth of the teacher's intentions can help the student develop confidence in the teacher and in the path: then the student can accept the teachings more easily.

O nce students have begun to follow the teachings, they usually think they will get something in return: a happier life, more friends, greater personal power. Yet even though it is true that Dharma practice produces many benefits, a student's particular desires may not be fulfilled. These expectations of where the spiritual path will lead seem reasonable and positive, but they make it difficult to accept the teachings because they color one's understanding. A student who holds fixed ideas about the teacher or the teachings is like an unclean jar that muddies whatever is poured into it. No matter how pure the teachings received by the student, they are clouded by prejudgment, and cannot be seen or understood clearly.

To help the student let go of his expectations, the teacher will encourage him to look at himself with complete honesty. This may not be easy, since a clear view requires cutting through layers of pride and self-doubt. But the teacher can see through these obscurations, and his vision helps the student to penetrate them. A relationship with a teacher thus provides an important opportunity to transform emotional attachments.

The teacher offers instructions which can lead to the same experiences and understanding he himself has gained. For the student, a traveler on the path to liberation, these teachings are a map, and the teacher is an experienced guide. It is the student's role to listen to the guide and to try to follow the map if he wishes to reach his destination. Though the teacher's oral and written instructions are just ideas and concepts, like symbols on a map, they are a means for reaching the destination. If we do not endeavor to follow the directions, the experience of realization may not come; we may wander off the path and lose our way.

A story about the great Tibetan yogi Milarepa illustrates how important it is to trust in the teacher and maintain a strong commitment. When Milarepa began to study with his teacher, Marpa, he was given very difficult tasks to accomplish, but the formal spiritual teachings which Milarepa sought were withheld. As each task was completed, Milarepa hoped that at last he would receive the teachings, but not only did Marpa refuse to give the teachings, he had Milarepa destroy his work and do it over again.

After many years had passed in this way, Milarepa began to think he could get the teachings he desired elsewhere. Knowing that the irascible Marpa would not willingly permit him to go, Milarepa left without Marpa's knowledge, and connived his way into being accepted by another teacher who gave Milarepa instructions that guaranteed enlightenment. Still, although Milarepa followed these instructions to the letter, he attained absolutely no result. The new teacher could not understand this—until he discovered that Milarepa had not finished his training with Marpa, and had in fact left without permission. Milarepa was promptly returned to Marpa. Eventually, when Marpa felt that his student was ready, Milarepa did receive the highest teachings, and in time became a supremely realized yogi.

This kind of commitment, requiring one to persevere for years, even in the absence of visible results, may be difficult to implement in today's world. Particularly in the West, where personal freedom is so highly valued, we may feel threatened by devotion: trusting someone so completely seems to jeopardize our independence.

For this reason, it can be helpful to look at the teacher from another perspective, as a symbol for the clarity and deep serenity that arise whenever we completely open our minds. Thus the term *guru* can refer to our internal awareness, our Buddha nature, and "surrendering to the guru" can mean opening to the enlightened quality of mind.

Still we may ask, "Is a personal teacher necessary to attain enlightenment?" The answer depends upon the individual. Most people can benefit from a relationship with an experienced teacher. There are those, however, who find such a relationship a hindrance: their fear of being manipulated blocks the instructions of a teacher. Such people find it easier to digest painful information about themselves at their own pace, on their own initiative. There are also rare individuals who can effectively direct their own development, and do not need a teacher at all.

While a teacher-student relationship may be advisable for most of us, a qualified teacher may not be easy to find in these days of confusion and conflict. Therefore, as we look for guidance, it is essential to evaluate a teacher carefully: Does he have a fully enlightened lineage? Is he willing to take responsibility for his students? An authentic teacher-student relationship is very different from relationships in which there is continuing dependence or manipulation. A genuine teacher is our true friend, willing to help us become absolutely free.

Watching the Watcher

*When you totally become the watcher,
it no longer exists as a separate entity.*

Student: When I was watching my thoughts, I would have the watcher watch my thoughts, and then I would watch the watcher.

Rinpoche:* I would like to listen carefully to what you are saying. Please, one word at a time.

Student: All right. When I had thoughts, I would watch the thoughts . . .

Rinpoche: When you have thoughts, then . . .

Student: . . . then I would remove myself from the thoughts and just watch them.

Rinpoche: Wait a minute. Again . . . when you have thoughts . . . you recognize there is a thought. Now, which one is the watcher?

*Rinpoche is a Tibetan title, meaning "most precious one." Here it refers to Tarthang Tulku.

Student: Well, what I was trying to do was to watch the watcher watching the thoughts.

Rinpoche: Okay, now what do you understand that to mean? Let's say that I am you. There is a thought. I watch that. Now what do I do? Which one is the watcher? Let's use very simple language. This is my thought, and I'm watching there [points to an object]. I am watching this thought. Now what do I do?

Student: The next thing I do is say, "*That's* not me. *This* is me."

Rinpoche: That's another thought!

Student: That's the problem.

Student 2: I think you should just look at the person that's watching.

Student: Yes, that was what I was trying to say. When I did that, I would feel much more spacious . . . a very peculiar feeling.

Rinpoche: All right. But as soon as you recognize a feeling, you are involved with a thought. If there is a recognition, then someone must be having that recognition.

Student: It's the one who is watching the thoughts, the one who perceives what is happening.

Rinpoche: Right. You need to jump *there*, chase the *face* of the watcher. That's all. Do you understand? Chase there, not somewhere else . . . in the very first moment . . . like chasing a tiger. When you are chasing his face, there is no second thought. When you chase completely, you become the experience. The chaser and the chased meet and immediately unite. No other thought is involved.

If you do this with all your thoughts, you will not miss anything.

More intellectually you may say, "My awareness recognizes." In this sense, your awareness has shape. It's like a shell, a specific form or a characteristic pattern with which you receive that thought. You need to chase that thought into this pattern or totality. The looker, receiver, perceiver, recognizer . . . just catch it! This immediately becomes the experience. There is no going 'this way' or 'that way', and nothing is left behind. Every thought is received into this totality. No other thought exists. At that time—at that very moment—your awareness instantly becomes illuminated. There are no divisions between things, no introducer and no introduced. That very first moment becomes the experience itself.

Normally, we think of thoughts as coming to us from somewhere else. For example, the recognizer catches a thought, which is felt to come from his mind. But while he seems to be chasing this thought, he is saying, "I am not the one who is chasing you, someone else is chasing you!" This is very tricky. Actually, the first thought is already gone, and the experiencer is creating another thought. The experiencer himself *is* the new thought. But the experiencer quietly insists, "I am not the one you want to look at, look over there." Actually, the one you need to catch is the one who is giving the answers, the one who tells you to look elsewhere. That's the one you need to chase and meet face to face. When you do successfully catch the thought, there is no longer any hunter or recognizer; the watcher has become the experience. By continuing this practice you can see that thoughts do not come from some other place.

Student: If I gave up trying to catch the thoughts that the recognizer is creating, would that be the same thing as catching a thought? I mean, suppose I gave up meditating entirely and forgot all this. Would I be at the same place?

Rinpoche: No. Perhaps you do not understand which thought you need to catch. I am trying to illustrate which one you need to bite into with your awareness. If you bite into the right thought, it has meaning and value. In effect, what you are saying is that whether you bite into the right thought or the wrong thought, your meditation is the same. It is not the same.

Let's say you're watching for a thought . . . "Oh, there's a thought. I can see it. I need to catch it." Meanwhile, another thought comes, because in order to catch it *your* way, there must be another thought. Otherwise you do not *think* you have caught it. That is your problem. You must create one thought in order to think you have caught another thought. After all, your logic says, if there is no hand, how can you grasp? Another thought is there—who catches it? Then another thought—who catches that one? In this way, your thoughts become split every which way. This can go on endlessly.

I will try to explain this a little differently. I say I see my thought. But actually, I am not seeing a thought separate from myself. There isn't any such thought *there*: the watcher is self-manifesting. The awareness is the awareness of a watcher, not of a thought apart from a watcher. The way I think about it and the way it is are two different things.

Within that moment when I seem to see my thought, I can interpret: there is a thought—I can feel it, see it, project it, and experience it happening. But the thought itself is actually not separate from the watcher. Between the thought and the watcher there are no gaps, no words or concepts, no second thoughts. When you directly face the watcher, your awareness and the watcher become one. The boundary which divides the subject from the object breaks open completely. All that is left is the experience itself, or, you might say, pure energy.

Now how do you break open that boundary? We must think about this very intelligently. Who sees? Who is experiencing? Just sit very quietly, gently go inside, and watch the thought. When you totally become the watcher, it no longer exists as a separate entity. *The thought disappears and the watcher disappears.* There is no separation or division, no subject or object. When this occurs, you naturally feel a surge of energy, a kind of shock . . . like a bubble that expands and expands until it pops. When you watch the watcher, there is no longer any thought form. All that is left is meditation . . . there is no subject, no object, no dual mind. The mind is totally silent.

Watching the watcher immediately and directly leads to a kind of light, or energy, or awareness. Just stay there. That is your meditation. If you try to go beyond that, you will create another thought.

When I'm talking, do you hear something? If so, then meditate on the hearer. Do you feel something? Then you can meditate on the feeler. Do you see something? Then meditate on the watcher. As your awareness develops naturally, you will begin to understand there is really no watching and no watcher.

Light of Awareness

This seeing energy changes the frozen energy
of emotion into pure awareness, just as
a ray of sunlight melts ice into water.

Reality is all-encompassing: the absolute nature is one. Although we may feel separate from the original uncreated reality—whether we call it "God," "peak experience," or "enlightened mind"—through awareness we can contact this essential part of ourselves.

Awareness forms the pure ground of our experience; it supports every aspect of our world with perfect equanimity. Its light can illuminate our experience and bring us complete understanding.

Like the smooth surface of a mirror, awareness reflects the sights and sounds of daily life. Just as a mirror and its image cannot be separated, pure awareness is not apart from everyday experience. Awareness infuses even the concepts and dualistic conditions set up by the mind. All apparently separate things are manifestations and categories within awareness.

Seeing only the images playing on the mirror's surface, we forget their origin; accepting as solid the elements of our world—thoughts, feelings, and perceptions—we lose sight of the underlying stream of awareness. But by focusing and slowing down the mind, we can begin to soften these rigid structures. Interesting new experiences may be discovered as awareness wells up to the surface.

Since awareness has the radiant quality of light and is linked to the sense of sight, many of the exercises that stimulate it involve vision and a sense of brightness. Here is one such exercise: Find a light, pleasant environment for your practice. Sitting comfortably, keep your eyes open without focusing on the objects in your visual field, and concentrate as though you were listening with your eyes to a distant sound. With practice, you will feel that you are able to hear with your eyes. Meditate directly within that silent, empty sound.

If you find this exercise difficult to do—you may feel your body growing tense or be bothered by many thoughts—close your eyes and relax in peaceful stillness before beginning again. A simple physical movement, such as rolling the head slowly from side to side, may also help clear your mind of distractions and thoughts.

Traditionally, when a student has gained some experience in meditation, his teacher introduces visualization exercises to stimulate awareness. The student might be asked to visualize a particular color or shape, or a religious image or symbol, depending on his disposition and the lineage of the teacher. In the practice the visualized object becomes a crystallization of awareness, suffusing body and mind with ecstatic clarity.

Visualization is a quick method for developing awareness, but it is not always easily accomplished. If you want to practice visualization, first choose an object to visualize; any simple and inspiring object or picture of an object can be used. Sitting comfortably, look directly at the object or picture. See it all at once, without following the specific features, as though you were looking at the face of a good friend. Look for a few minutes, then close your eyes and watch the after-image of the object. When it fades, open your eyes and look at the object again. Spend several meditation sessions doing this until you are familiar with the object.

Then, with your eyes open, picture the object several feet in front of you, either directly in front of the body, or at eye level. See the image distinctly, but do not strain. If you cannot see it clearly at first, or if the image fades in and out of your visual field, concentrate on the feeling aroused by the image rather than its form. Make this sense of the object's presence as intense as possible. Know with certainty that the object is there. As you directly touch this knowing feeling, your whole body becomes transformed into a state of relaxation. There is no longer the impression of a specific experience; you are completely surrounded by awareness. Feeling the object intensely in this way is a preliminary to seeing it clearly. Eventually, the image will emerge as a clear and vibrant expression of awareness.

You can then visualize the object either in front of your body or within your body. Or you can alternate, first seeing the image in front of you, then drawing it within yourself, then seeing it in front again. Shifting the visualization like this until the movement is easily accomplished will add a flexible precision to your awareness.

At the close of your practice, let the visualization dissolve completely into pure awareness. This may be done by allowing the image to move away from you and grow smaller and smaller, until it is barely visible in the distance. This tiny speck then merges into pure light. Remain as long as possible in the silent space that visualization has opened.

As your practice gains momentum, you will find the visualization image appearing spontaneously throughout the day. Your consciousness becomes charged with a "seeing" quality that dissolves most emotional problems and negative patterns as soon as they appear.

When very intense emotions arise, you can use your visualization image as a tool. At these times look at the image directly, bringing the awareness it evokes into each thought and feeling. This seeing energy changes the frozen energy of emotion into pure awareness, just as a ray of sunlight melts ice into water.

In time, the visualization image itself will come to be recognized as pure awareness: the image is perfectly present, and perfectly open. Through sustained practice this understanding will gradually extend, so that we see its clarity within each and every object. We will see how our 'world' arises from and returns to this lucid dimension. As we attend to the light while focusing the energies of our body and mind, our whole being can wake up and merge into a brilliant, unified field of awareness.

Dream and Illusion

*Once we truly understand that our
waking experience is dreamlike, we no longer
have to treat life as a serious problem.*

When we awaken from a nightmare, we are filled
with relief to learn it was only a dream. The fear
subsides, and as the shapes and forms of familiar
reality emerge, we can look back and laugh at how
scared we were by the illusion. Yet our waking reality,
though perhaps more rational and familiar, is no more
substantial than a dream. Even its most solid and vivid
aspects are devoid of real substance.

The teachings of dream yoga show us how to see the
dreamlike quality of waking reality. But why, if our lives
are comfortable, would we want to do this? As long as
our experience is positive and we are not shaken by some
outside cause, we are content to accept life as it is, lulled
by its seemingly pleasant nature. But when it becomes
threatening, and we feel our problems closing in on us,
we struggle for freedom, just as in a bad dream.

Our usual perspective on life shows that the whole
world has problems, and each individual has his or her

own particular difficulties. Some situations are uncomfortable, unbalanced, or dissatisfying . . . maybe often, or all the time. But dream yoga teaches us that these problems exist because we believe in this reality that we have created, and think that it is an objective fact.

We adopt certain ideas about the self, happiness, success, love, and so on, and then take our creations seriously, considering them real and unchangeable. When life contradicts our preconceptions, we struggle and suffer. Thus our willingness to believe in a substantial and stable reality ironically makes us victims of life's evanescence.

Once we truly understand that our waking experience is dreamlike, we no longer have to treat life as a serious problem. We can relax and become more flexible, because the reality of a dream is not very solid or permanent. Our personality changes and our relationships with other people and the world improve.

In understanding waking reality as a dream, dream yoga is not concerned with the interpretation of experience. We can talk endlessly about meanings behind experiences, but these are indirect understandings and are not of prime importance. Instead, dream yoga tries to discover what reality is *directly*, by merging the waking state and the dream state.

Looking at our lives as a whole, we see that we were born, we grew up, went to school, and worked; we have the same body, the same mind, perhaps the same interests. But our lives up to now exist only as the reflections of past memories. Memory seems to be the only way we can verify past experience. And if we look carefully, we see that these memory patterns are very similar in quality to nighttime dreams.

Likewise, we may examine our experience of the dream state. Commonly we think that a dream is unreal, untrue, impermanent. But unless you are very aware within a dream, the experience of night-dreaming seems to be 'real' . . . the same as now.

We may think there is a wall between the two sides—between 'real' and 'unreal', day-dreaming and night-dreaming—but any kind of experience we can have on one side, we can have on the other. We may try to discriminate, and say, "*This* is a day-dream," but the difference lies only in our minds, in the statement we are making. When we take away our mental wall, day-dreaming and night-dreaming, real and unreal, become one.

The following exercise can help you find the link between dreams and waking reality, and allow you to extend meditation to your dreams. It is done as you fall asleep, either during the day or at night. Breathe softly and evenly, and let your head, neck, and all your muscles relax. Let everything slow down, so that your mind becomes very calm. Without making an effort, watch how the mental images begin and end. Do not concentrate on them too tightly or you may not fall asleep. While delicately observing the mind, lead it gently into the dream state, as though you were leading a child by the hand.

Watch the dream without losing your 'waking awareness'. This is not difficult; in fact, most of us have experienced this awareness in past dreams. It often arises when a dream is disturbing, and events in it are growing more threatening. At this point some aspect of our consciousness tells us not to worry—the experience is only a dream—and the dream is no longer frightening.

When you can relax within your dream, realizing that you are asleep, you have gained control of dreaming. Then you can do almost anything in your dreams. You can fly, travel to exciting places, have whatever experience you can imagine in this ever-changing state.

ext you can learn to see the flexibility and openness of dream life within your waking experience. Relax and feel the light, mobile energy of the dream state. Look upon all your experience directly as a dream; this can be very enjoyable and interesting. Walking, talking, drinking, eating—everything is within the dream. Do not try to change anything, or *imagine* that ordinary experience is a dream; just be loose and relaxed. Whatever arises, whatever you feel, simply accept it as another image in the dream. You can even view yourself, your consciousness, as a part of the dream. Though you are the projector creating the images, you are also a part of the picture. Realize that the dreamlike nature of existence includes every aspect of being—even enlightenment is a part of the dream.

If you practice seeing everything as being equally within the dream, you cultivate a healthy, balanced mind. However, you may think, "If I accept that everything's a dream, I might quit working, and just try to enjoy myself all the time." But seeing life as a dream is no reason to change anything, because whatever you're doing is *already* part of the dream. There's nothing we can hide, nothing we can secretly do that is not part of the dream. All we need to do is watch it.

Many times the Buddha indicated that the world is like an illusion. Once we realize this, even the most difficult and painful situations do not cause us to lose balance, and beautiful and desirable things fail to encourage attachment or grasping. Because our problems no longer control us, we are free to help others with their difficulties. When we see the dreamlike nature of reality, we are no longer controlled by the illusion of ordinary experience. We are free to fully appreciate the play of life's images.

Preparation for Understanding Shunyata

*Everything is existing perfectly
as complete openness.*

When we first consider the possibility of becoming enlightened, we understand enlightenment as some separate *form* of experience. We assume that meditation leads to higher and lighter states of being, until finally everything changes somehow from what we normally see and feel to an experience of continual joy and bliss. But from the viewpoint of the highest realization, whatever we are involved in is already within enlightenment. Everything is already perfect; not one single imperfect thing exists, no 'thing' needs cleaning or developing. Each form, each specific quality is already complete in being whatever it is, just as it is.

From this perspective there is no nonenlightenment and no enlightenment, no samsara and no nirvana. The intrinsic perfection of existence is beyond all relative interpretations or attempts to describe its qualities. Even before we begin to practice and meditate, all appearances and forms are manifestations of perfect being. Thus there is nothing to gain, nothing to lose, nothing to realize, and nowhere to go.

Then why are we not already enlightened? How can we be within perfect existence when our world and our lives seem so far from utopia?

The answers to these questions lie in our tendency to give everything an identity, and label, define, and categorize all our experience. Through this process we lose touch with reality, for as soon as we start to describe and interpret, we are outside, looking *at it*. By standing apart from reality, we create the separation which we then try to bridge with our meditation.

We even think about realization as the goal of a subject-object relationship, not seeing that this "realization" is merely another concept, a product of our conditioning that obscures the potential depth and clarity of the mind. In truth, there is nothing to discover in either the subject or the object—no space, no time, no matter; there is not even any mind.

Then who can realize enlightenment? No one. There is no 'I', no experiencer, and no experience. Everything is existing perfectly as complete openness. All manifestations are emptiness and emptiness is all manifestations. Yet we—as individuals—cannot grasp this perfect openness. We cannot see it, touch it, smell it, interpret or experience it: there is no 'me' to grasp, to see, smell, or experience, to deny or affirm the physicality of material substance, or even to make the comparison between existent or nonexistent.

Absolute openness, or shunyata, has nothing to stand on; it has no position. With neither characteristics nor essence, it cannot be experienced by the senses or by the mind. Yet nothing is outside shunyata. Reality includes all positions, every aspect of existence and nonexistence. In shunyata there is room for every possibility, and everything fits perfectly.

You begin to understand emptiness when you cut out preconceptions. If you believe shunyata is a tremendous expanse, discard this idea. If you believe in mind, or that everything is mind-created, or that there is some foundation or substance, throw away such a concept. Unmask everything and let your mind become totally silent, peaceful, empty, and clear: let it *become* the experience of shunyata. Within this clear and empty space between thoughts, before another concept forms, there is no subject, no object, and no experience. Here is the nature of enlightenment.

This may be hard to accept if we have an inaccurate concept of enlightenment. We may think that attaining enlightenment requires more than simply embracing the open quality of emptiness. But our *ideas* of enlightenment and infinite beings are often restrictive. We have created these concepts to better understand our reality, yet ironically these very concepts can block our realization.

We also create restrictions by considering ourselves separate from other things. We think that we reach out to touch something apart from ourselves, or that we look around to see something outside, but the toucher is already touching, the looker is already seeing. As soon as we postulate something as separate, or isolate something in order to try to understand it, we lose sight of shunyata.

W here does the mind come from? Where does it go? Where is the source of consciousness? Where does life originate? Where is all existence created? The answer to all these questions is *nowhere*; it is all the same reality, the same energy, without source or beginning. There is no real separation between past and present, here and there. We are always within reality. Our mind is not separate from enlightenment.

What then is the difference between enlightenment and ordinary existence? The enlightened state has great richness, openness, and fullness of being, while the samsaric state has tremendous suffering, ignorance, and confusion. Nevertheless, from the standpoint of shunyata, the two states coexist; there is no separation between them.

When we understand that the foundation of enlightenment is not any place or any person, we will know that we have never been apart from this awakened mind. We will see that enlightenment permeates our entire being and can no more be separated from us than sound can be divorced from music. Shunyata is nothing and everything. All our experience is included within this perfect realization of openness.

Index

Other Dharma Publishing Books

Time, Space, and Knowledge: A New Vision of Reality by Tarthang Tulku. Thirty-five exercises and a rigorous philosophical text reveal ever more brilliant times, spaces, and knowledges.

Kum Nye Relaxation, Parts 1 and 2 by Tarthang Tulku. Over 200 exercises for discovering the relaxing energies within our bodies and senses.

Gesture of Balance by Tarthang Tulku. The Nyingma method of meditation wherein all life experience is meditation.

Openness Mind by Tarthang Tulku. The sequel to *Gesture of Balance*, with more advanced meditation techniques.

Skillful Means by Tarthang Tulku. A manual for making work a source of unlimited fulfillment.

Kindly Bent to Ease Us by Longchenpa. A translation of Longchenpa's guide to the Dzogchen path to enlightenment.

The Life and Liberation of Padmasambhava by Yeshe Tsogyal. A translation of the complete biography of Tibetan Buddhism's founder. Two volumes, 58 color plates.

Crystal Mirror Series edited by Tarthang Tulku. Introductory exploration of the various aspects of Tibetan philosophy, history, psychology, art, and culture. Five volumes currently available.

Calm and Clear by Lama Mipham. Translations of two beginning meditation texts by a brilliant 19th century Tibetan Lama.

If you order Dharma books directly from the publisher, it will help us to make more such books available. Write for a free catalog and new book announcements.

Dharma Publishing   2425 Hillside Avenue
Berkeley, California 94704   USA